Animals All Around

Do Penguins Have Puppies?

A Book About Animal Babies

Written by Michael Dahl

Illustrated by Sandra D'Antonio

Content Consultant: Kathleen E. Hunt, Ph.D.
Research Scientist and Lecturer, Zoology Department
University of Washington, Seattle, Washington

Reading Consultant: Susan Kesselring, M.A., Literacy Educator
Rosemount-Apple Valley-Eagan (Minnesota) School District

PICTURE WINDOW BOOKS
MINNEAPOLIS, MINNESOTA

Animals All Around series editor: Peggy Henrikson
Page production: The Design Lab
The illustrations in this book were rendered in marker.

Picture Window Books
151 Good Counsel Drive
P.O. Box 669
Mankato, MN 56002-0669
1-877-845-8392
www.picturewindowbooks.com

Printed in the United States of America.

 All books published by Picture Window Books
are manufactured with paper containing at least
10 percent post-consumer waste.

Library of Congress Cataloging-in-Publication Data
Dahl, Michael.
Do penguins have puppies? / written by Michael Dahl ; illustrated by
Sandra D'Antonio.
p. cm. — (Animals all around)
Includes bibliographical references and index.
Summary: Introduces the offspring of a number of different
animals.
ISBN 978-1-4048-0102-8 (library binding)
ISBN 978-1-4048-0372-5 (paperback)
1. Animals—Infancy—Juvenile literature. [1. Parental behavior
in animals. 2. Animals—Infancy.] I. D'Antonio, Sandra, 1956— ill.
II. Title.
QL763 .D3 2003
599.13'9—dc21
2002155002

No! Dogs have puppies.

A group of puppies born at the same time to the same mother is called a litter. A large litter can have 12 or more puppies in it. Puppies in the same litter are called littermates.

Do penguins have calves?

No! Cows have calves.

Calves can stand up and walk soon after they are born. Calves frolic in grassy meadows. Sometimes they stop to sniff the trees and flowers. They follow their mothers as the cows wander and graze.

Do penguins have fawns?

No! Deer have fawns.

Fawns are born in the spring. They have reddish coats and white spots on their backs to help them hide. The fawns blend in with the forest flowers and splashes of spring sunlight.

8

Do penguins have kittens?

No! Cats have kittens.

Newborn kittens are born with closed ears and eyes. A kitten's eyes take a few weeks to fully open. A mother cat keeps her kittens close by her side, protecting and feeding them.

Do penguins have goslings?

No! Geese have goslings.

Baby geese are born with tiny flaps of skin between their toes. These webbed feet help the goslings paddle and swim when they are just a few days old.

Do penguins have cubs?

No! Bears have cubs.

Bear cubs are born in the middle of winter. Little cubs stay with their mother inside their sleeping place, called a den. In spring, the cubs leave the den for the first time to play and explore.

Do penguins have joeys?

No! Kangaroos have joeys.

Baby kangaroos, called joeys, are about half the size of a grape when they are born. At birth, the tiny joeys crawl into their mother's pouch. Here they stay safe and warm for many weeks, until they are big enough to hop on their own.

Do penguins have tadpoles?

No! Frogs have tadpoles.

Baby frogs are called tadpoles when they hatch from their eggs. Tadpoles have small, round heads and long tails. They wiggle in the water like little fish. After a while, the tadpoles grow legs and become frogs like their parents.

Do penguins have foals?

No!
Horses
have foals.

Baby horses, called foals, can stand an hour or two after they are born. Soon they are running, jumping, and playing. Foals also have a good sense of smell. A foal can find its mother by her smell.

Do penguins have chicks?

Yes! Penguins have chicks.

Penguin chicks grow up fast where freezing breezes blow and blast. Feathers grow quickly and keep chicks warm in the wild sea or a winter storm.

Animal Babies

Some animal babies look like their mothers.

calves	cows
fawns	deer
foals	horses

Some animal babies look different from their mothers.

tadpoles	frogs

Some animal babies hatch from eggs.

goslings	geese
chicks	penguins

Some animal babies are born in the open air.

puppies	dogs
kittens	cats
cubs	bears
joeys	kangaroos

Words to Know

coat—the hair or fur on some animals' bodies. Fawns have spotted coats.

den—a place where a bear sleeps. A bear's den might be a cave or hollow tree.

graze—to move about and eat grass and other plants. Cows graze in the meadow.

hatch—to break out of a shell. Goslings, tadpoles, and penguin chicks hatch from eggs.

litter—a group of baby animals all born at the same time to the same mother. Dogs and cats have litters.

pouch—a special pocket on a mother kangaroo's tummy for holding her babies

webbed feet—feet with flaps of skin between the toes. Goslings are born with webbed feet to help them swim.

Index

To Learn More

At the Library

Knox, Barbara. *Baby Animals 1, 2, 3: A Counting Book of Animal Offspring.* Mankato, Minn.: A+ Books, 2003.

Longenecker, Theresa. *Who Grows Up On the Farm? A Book About Farm Animals and Their Offspring.* Minneapolis: Picture Window Books, 2003.

Longenecker, Theresa. *Who Grows Up in the Forest? A Book About Forest Animals and Their Offspring.* Minneapolis: Picture Window Books, 2003.

Simon, Seymour. *Baby Animals.* New York: SeaStar Books, 2002.

On the Web

FactHound offers a safe, fun way to find Web sites related to topics in this book. All of the sites on FactHound have been researched by our staff.

1. Visit www.facthound.com

2. Type in this special code: 1404801022

3. Click on the FETCH IT button.

Your trusty FactHound will fetch the best Web sites for you!